The UNIVERSE

Mary Kay Carson

Rourke
Educational Media

rourkeeducationalmedia.com

Scan for Related Titles

Teaching Focus:

Text features: Labels and Captions- How do the labels and captions help you as you read this book?

Before Reading:

Building Academic Vocabulary and Background Knowledge

Before reading a book, it is important to set the stage for your child or student by using pre-reading strategies. This will help them develop their vocabulary, increase their reading comprehension, and make connections across the curriculum.

1. Read the title and look at the cover. *Let's make predictions about what this book will be about.*
2. Take a picture walk by talking about the pictures/photographs in the book. Implant the vocabulary as you take the picture walk. Be sure to talk about the text features such as headings, Table of Contents, glossary, bolded words, captions, charts/diagrams, or Index.
3. Have students read the first page of text with you then have students read the remaining text.
4. Strategy Talk – use to assist students while reading.
   - Get your mouth ready
   - Look at the picture
   - Think…does it make sense
   - Think…does it look right
   - Think…does it sound right
   - Chunk it – by looking for a part you know
5. Read it again.
6. After reading the book complete the activities below.

Content Area Vocabulary
Use glossary words in a sentence.

Big Bang
galaxy
matter
orbit
supercluster
telescope

After Reading:

Comprehension and Extension Activity

After reading the book, work on the following questions with your child or students in order to check their level of reading comprehension and content mastery.

1. *Describe the Big Bang.* (Summarize)
2. *Is a supercluster larger or smaller than a galaxy? Explain.* (Asking questions)
3. *What galaxy do we live in?* (Text to self connection)
4. *What makes up a universe?* (Summarize)

Extension Activity

The universe includes everything: stars, planets, and galaxies. Write a poem that describes the universe. Be sure to include descriptive words and science words like stars, gravity, comets, planets, moons, or ice.

Table of Contents

Your Universe

The universe is everything that's anywhere. Everything that exists is part of the universe, from stars and planets to the anthill outside your school.

Billions of galaxies make up the universe. It includes all the stars and planets. Gases, dust, and energy are out in space, too. The universe is a big place. Where do you live in it? And what else is out there?

Scientists estimate that the observable universe is more

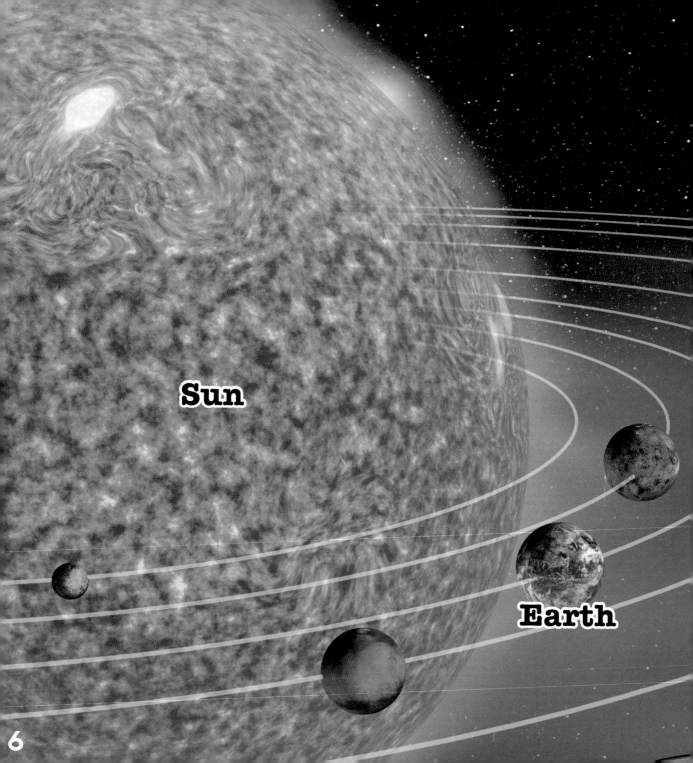

Sun

Earth

Our Sun and Nearby Neighbors

The night sky is a blanket of stars. Stars are balls of hot, glowing gases. The star closest to Earth is the Sun. It's the center of our solar system. Earth and the other planets circle, or **orbit**, the Sun.

The Sun is a medium-sized yellow star. There are billions of others like it in the universe. Scientists have even found an Earth-like planet! Could planets like Earth have life?

Kepler was launched into space in 2009. It is a space **telescope**. *Kepler* zooms in on the stars in the night sky. It looks for planets orbiting those stars. *Kepler* has found more than 900 new planets!

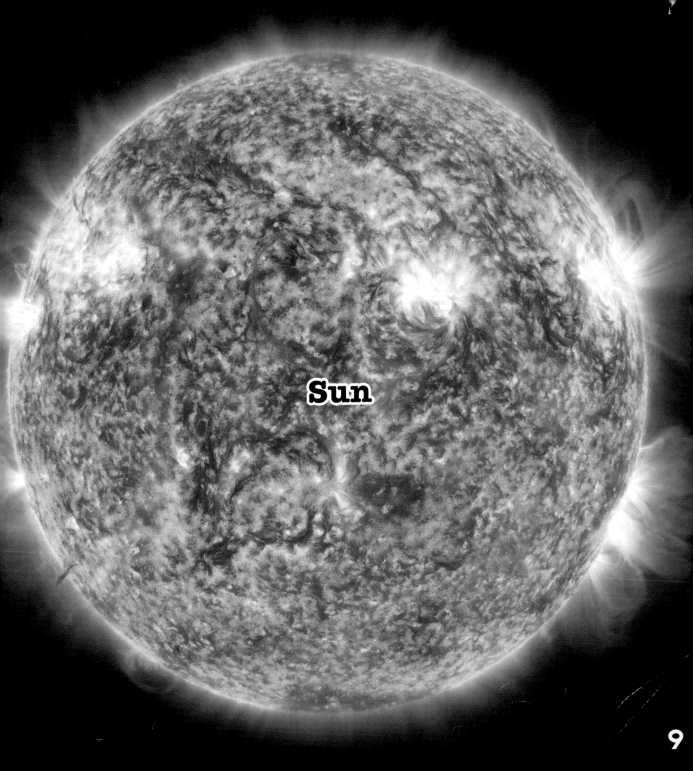

Sun

Galactic Clusters

Our solar system is part of the Milky Way **galaxy**. A galaxy is a group of stars with a shape. The Milky Way is a spiral galaxy. It is home to at least 100 billion stars.

When conditions are right, you can see the arm of our Milky Way galaxy from Earth.

The Milky Way is one of thirty galaxies in the Local Group. The Milky Way and Andromeda galaxies are the Local Group's two biggest.

Andromeda

Andromeda has four times as many stars as the Milky Way. It's bright enough to see in the night sky.

The Hubble Space Telescope took this picture. There are more than 10,000 galaxies in it. Some are the farthest galaxies ever seen.

Superclusters and Cosmic Voids

A group of galaxies forms a **supercluster**. About 1,000 galaxies make up the Virgo Supercluster.

As you zoom out, the universe gets less even. Stringy, lumpy patches of galaxies clump together and are surrounded by empty space.

These voids are like bubbles. Galaxies clump on the outside of them, like soapy froth.

The Milky Way is in the Virgo Supercluster, along with all the other Local Group galaxies. So is this bright spiral galaxy called NGC 2997.

Telescopes are the tools of space scientists. Some telescopes collect visible light, like a camera. Other telescopes gather invisible light, like ultraviolet and x-rays. These telescopes help scientists learn more about the objects they are studying.

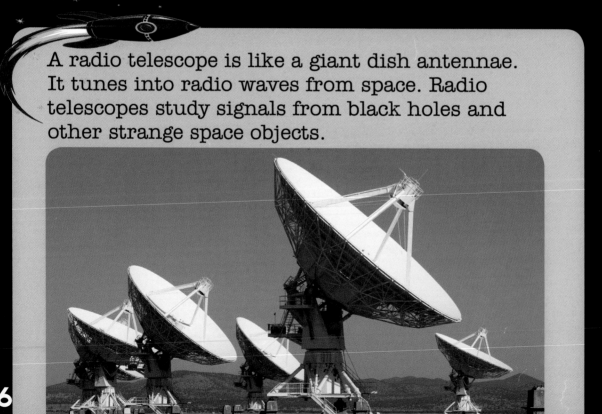

A radio telescope is like a giant dish antennae. It tunes into radio waves from space. Radio telescopes study signals from black holes and other strange space objects.

Engineers wear clean suits while building spacecraft, like the *James Webb Space Telescope*. It is set to launch in 2018.

Our Growing Universe

Scientists think the **Big Bang** started it all. This explosion created the universe about 13.7 billion years ago.

The young universe was hot and tightly-packed. As it cooled, it spread out. Material clumped into galaxies.

The universe is still expanding, or spreading out, faster as it ages. Why is this happening? Scientists think it might be a mysterious dark energy.

Another puzzle for scientists is dark **matter.** It's an invisible substance that is more common than regular matter.

Most of the universe is invisible and not understood. Imagine the discoveries to come!

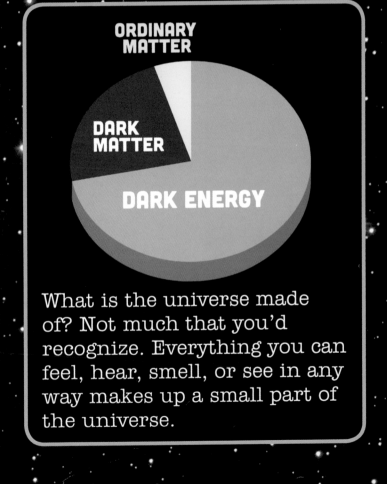

ORDINARY MATTER

DARK MATTER

DARK ENERGY

What is the universe made of? Not much that you'd recognize. Everything you can feel, hear, smell, or see in any way makes up a small part of the universe.

Photo Glossary

Big Bang (BIG BANG): A theory that the universe began and expanded after a powerful explosion of a tiny amount of dense matter.

galaxy (GAL-uhk-see): A large group of stars held together into a shape by gravity.

matter (MAT-ur): Matter is any kind of substance that takes up space.

orbit (OR-bit): The path traveled by a space object around another object.

supercluster (SOO-pur-KLUHSS-tur): Galaxies that have clumped together.

telescope (TEL-uh-skope): An instrument used by scientists to make distant objects appear larger.

Index

Websites

http://amazing-space.stsci.edu/
http://chandra.harvard.edu/edu/
http://starchild.gsfc.nasa.gov

Meet The Author!
www.meetREMauthors.com

About the Author

Mary Kay Carson has written more than a dozen nonfiction books for children about space topics, including the *Far-Out Guide to the Solar System* series, *Exploring the Solar System*, and *Beyond the Solar System*. Two of her books have received the Children's Literature Award from the American Institute of Aeronautics and Astronautics.

www.rourkeeducationalmedia.com

PHOTO CREDITS: Cover, title page and page 4 © Vadim Sadovski; p 5 © ESO/M. Kornmesser, http://www.eso.org/public/images/eso12(page 4 inset © S1001; page 6-7 © Orla; page 8 courtesy NASA, 9 © Triff; page 10-11 © John A Davis; page 12 © Viktar Malyshchyts, pag courtesy NASA; page 15 eso1042f ©ESO/P. Grosbøl www.eso.org/ lic/images/eso1042f/ page 16 © fstockfoto, page 17 credit: NASA/(Gunn; page 18 © Igor Zh., page 19 courtesy NASA; page 20-21 © I Chekalin; page 22 top to bottom © Igor Zh., eso1042f ©ESO/P. Gro www.eso.org/public/images/eso1042f/, S1001; page 23 top to bott Orla, NASA, Master3D

Edited by Jill Sherman

Cover design and Interior design by Nicola Stratford nicolastratford.c

Library of Congress PCN Data

The Universe / Mary Kay Carson
(Inside Outer Space)
ISBN 978-1-62717-731-3 (hard cover)
ISBN 978-1-62717-853-2 (soft cover)
ISBN 978-1-62717-965-2 (e-Book)
Library of Congress Control Number: 2014935657

Rourke Educational Media
Printed in the United States of America, North Mankato, Minnesota

Also Available as:
ROURKE'S
e-Book